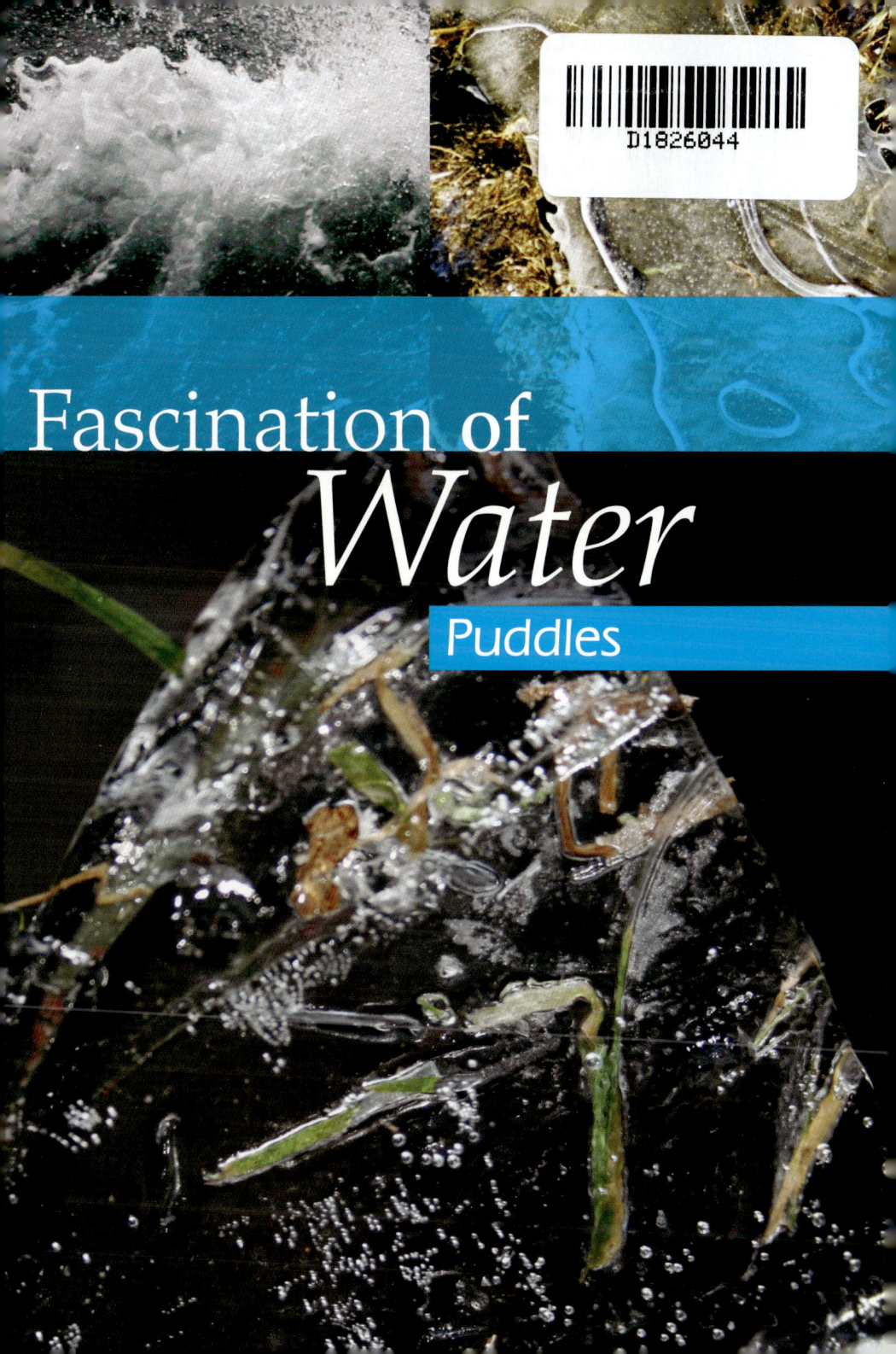

Fascination of
Water

Puddles

Many thanks to Dan Phillips, Kate Hookham, Steven White and Petra Babikova, for their contribution and in making this book possible.

Special thanks go to all the children for whom we are in contact with on a daily basis for their joy and inspiration.

© Claire Warden 2011
First published 2013

The rights of Claire Warden to be identified as the author of this work have been asserted in accordance with the Copyright Designs and Patents Act 1988

Design and layout by Almond www.almondtds.com +44 (0)131 553 5523

Printed by J. Thomson Colour Printers, Glasgow, UK

Photography by Claire Warden and the Kindergarten teams.

All photographs © Mindstretchers Ltd 2013

ISBN 978-1-906116-13-2

For further information about Mindstretchers publications and the full range of learning resources, email enquiries@mindstretchers.co.uk

Glenruthven Mill
Abbey Road
Auchterarder
PH3 1DP
Scotland, UK

T: +44 (0)1764 664409
F: +44 (0)1764 660728
E: enquiries@mindstretchers.co.uk
www.mindstretchers.com

Foreword
by Sally York
Education Policy Advisor for Forestry Commission Scotland

You need time to play in puddles. It is one of those delights on a walk to discover a puddle and explore it; how deep, how wide, how big a splash? I love it when the puddles are frozen as the patterns are always different, and then there is the noise when you stand on the ice and it starts to fracture! The mud associated with puddles, offers endless opportunities for 'guddling' about. At the simplest level just stomping through it, making patterns with your wellies, and depending on the viscosity of the mud, seeing how long the patterns stay. 'Mud, mud glorious mud', (otherwise known as the Hippopotamus Song by Flanders and Swann), sums up the pleasure of muddy puddles. Mind you, there are many times when it doesn't go near the shear pleasure of mud!

Moreover, this is a very precious resource in life, not least when working with children. They need the time to explore the wonder of the world around them, that to tired adult eyes can sometimes seem like messing about. It is this 'messing about' that has such tremendous learning potential in many different ways, and that is essential for children, especially these days where their lives can be so driven by adult timetables.

There is a wonderful poem by W.H. Davies, written in 1911 called 'Leisure'. It starts with: 'What is this life if full of care we have no time to stand and stare'.

As adults, we have to make the time to 'stand and stare' with children, as they open up the endless possibilities of the world around them. It is in these instances that learning becomes child led, but not just that, it can be that time stands still as we hark back to those initial fascinations we had as a child. It can open our eyes to the amazing world around us and allow us to see it through a child's eyes again. In my mind, there is nothing more important these days than to take the time to rediscover the fascination of something like 'guddling' in puddles with a child, to realise what is important in this world.

This book is a fascination in its own right. It is a great way to expose puddles in the way we need to record our work with children. It is an even better way to rediscover the sheer pleasure of puddles. Take the time to 'stand and stare' with young children around puddles and prepare to be amazed!

Contents

Introduction

Puddles are one of the most wonderful play materials that nature can provide. It is wonderful to see children meet a puddle for the first time and see it with such awe and wonder, adults can see them through a different lens. The question for us as practitioners and educators is: how do we start to reveal the possibilities of something as simple as a puddle, that belies such complex learning?

This series of books, is my way of starting to reveal the opportunities for children to learn with nature, not about it or by sitting in it, but by connecting to it, to take messages from it and start to ponder their significance in terms of the larger issues that face us in modern society, such as sustainability. I do hope that you enjoy the stories of how children have explored puddles and start to see the huge amount of learning that takes place in the process.

C. Warden.

Claire Warden 2013

Chapter 1. What is a puddle?

A puddle is a small accumulation of liquid, usually water on a surface. It can form either by pooling in a depression on the surface, or by surface tension upon a flat surface. Puddles are usually formed from rainwater or from irrigation.

A puddle tends to be small enough for an adult to step across, shallow enough to walk through, and too small to traverse in a boat. Puddles can be a source of fascination for children, as well as attracting other small wildlife!

There are many people who have used the word puddle to create new and interesting phrases that can lead to wonderful language work with children. Words such as 'puddle jumper', a name given for short duration flights between lakes on sea planes; a 'puddle light', for the light at the bottom of a car door and 'puddle suits', for the waterproofs worn by children.

Natural puddles and nature's use

Puddles in natural landscapes and habitats can indicate the presence of a spring. In medieval times, these natural springs were often 'helped' along by lining a depression with naturally occurring clay to create a feature, like a small round puddle or pond. Historical accounts around the world, often mention cultural respect for clean water, where each drop of water was used and considered valuable.

Wildlife uses puddles as a drinking source for bathing, for example birds, or in the case of some smaller life such as tadpoles, an entire habitat. Raised constructed puddles, such as bird baths, are a part of many domestic and wildlife gardens as a garden ornament and 'micro-habitat' restoration. A huge variety of life can exist in a puddle of water.

Small seasonal plants, grasses and wildflowers can germinate with a small amount of water in the ground, which is just enough moisture to start germination. In environments such as the temperate north, where there is rain all year round, the fringes of the puddle can often be the area that is colonised by small grasses.

How are puddles formed and where do they go?

Water cycle

Our planet is fortunate in that it has the capacity to recycle water to clean it (as much as it can). Water is delayed from entering the ground water level, when there is a barrier to its flow to the sea level. Puddles are a holding point for water as they can last for minutes or days, depending on the climatic conditions and the nature of the soil.

The water cycle refers to the continuous exchange of water within the hydrosphere, between the atmosphere, soil water, surface water, groundwater, and plants.

Water moves perpetually through each of these regions in the water cycle consisting of following transfer processes:

- Evaporation from oceans and other water bodies into the air and transpiration from land plants and animals into air
- Precipitation from water vapour condensing from the air and falling to the earth or ocean
- Run-off from the land and usually reaching the sea

Most water vapour over the oceans returns to the oceans, but winds carry water vapor over land at the same rate as run-off into the sea. Over land, evaporation and transpiration contribute to its return. Precipitation, during the year over land, has several forms: in our temperate climate of Scotland it falls most commonly as rain, snow, and hail, with some contribution from fog and dew. Water droplets in the air can refract sunlight to produce rainbows.

Water run-off often collects over watersheds flowing into rivers. Some of the water is diverted to irrigation for agriculture. Rivers and seas offer opportunity for travel and commerce. Through erosion, run-off shapes the environment creating river valleys and deltas which provide rich soil and level ground for the establishment of population centres.

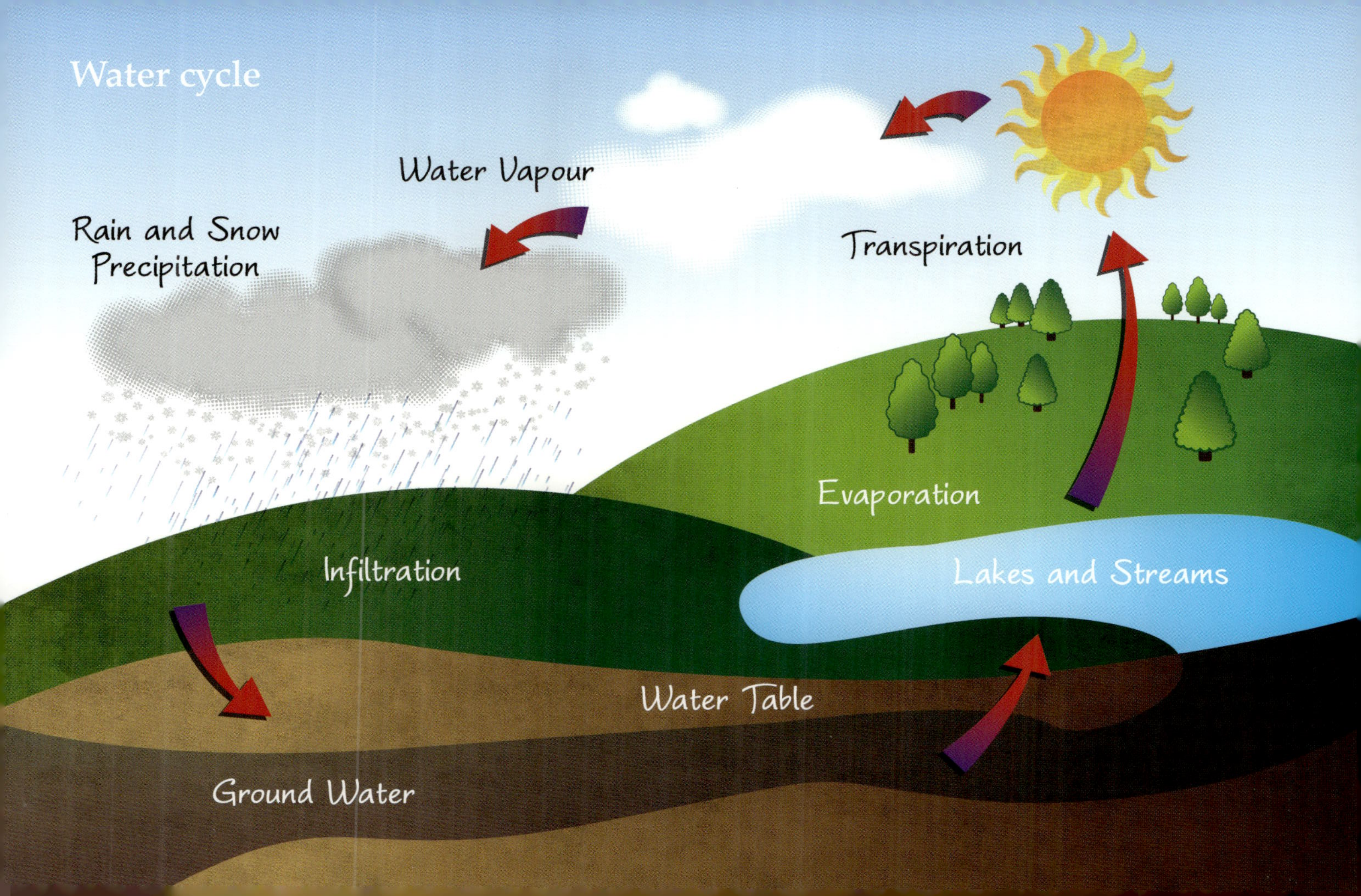

Water cycle

Water Vapour

Rain and Snow
Precipitation

Transpiration

Evaporation

Lakes and Streams

Water Table

Infiltration

Ground Water

Surface tension

The most obvious element of a puddle is the surface and how it varies over a day, a week, or through the seasons. It is this feature that attracts attention before the shape of the outline as it reflects the light. Children find puddles exciting all year round, however, there are few people who can resist cracking the ice on puddles. Watching and hearing the ice crack, whilst observing the muddy water seep up, is a favourite aspect of going on long walks at the Nature Kindergarten.

Water tension is caused by the cohesion of water molecules. The water molecules in the main body of the liquid can pull equally by the other water molecules around it. The molecules at the upper level of the water only have molecules pulling them downwards, so creating a surface tension.

The surface tension of a liquid is measured in something called dynes. The dynes required to break the surface tension of water is 72.

The existence of surface tension can be explored in many ways, from looking at water when in a clear container, to a rain drop on a 'Lady's Mantle' leaf, to floating objects on the top of the water, such as petals and grasses.

Fascinations over the years

Puddles are often a source of fascination by children, who regard jumping in puddles as an 'up-side' to rain. A number of examples of this fascination are demonstrated in this book. The fascination for puddle exploration has been recorded throughout time, and a good example is a children's nursery rhyme which records the story of Doctor Foster and his encounter with a puddle in Gloucester.

> *'Doctor Foster went to Gloucester*
> *In a shower of rain.*
> *He stepped in a puddle*
> *Right up to his middle*
> *And never went there again!'*

The origins and history of the poem, 'Doctor Foster' are in the United Kingdom and this is made clear with the reference to the southern county of Gloucestershire (Doctor Foster went to Gloucester ...). The rhyme was a warning to children in bygone days, prior to modern roads, which may appear to be a shallow puddle and could in fact, be much deeper!

A medieval legend originating from the UK, spoke of one man who was desperate to find building materials for his house, stole cobblestones from the road surface. The remaining hole filled with water, and a horseman who later walked through the 'puddle' actually found himself drowning. A similar legend is of a young boy drowning in a puddle that formed in a chuckhole (a pothole), in a major street in the early years of Seattle, USA, and is still told in areas of this region today.

When Walter Raleigh met Queen Elizabeth I, Raleigh is reputed to have thrown his coat over a muddy puddle to allow the Queen to cross without getting her feet wet. Such activities were once part of chivalry, but are less common nowadays!

Puddles have formed much fascination over the years for children and adults alike, so much so, that a theory was devised known as 'Puddle' theory by Douglas Adams to satirise the 'Fine-tuned Universe' argument for supernatural creationism. As quoted in Richard Dawkins' eulogy for Douglas Adams:

'... imagine a puddle waking up one morning and thinking, "This is an interesting world I find myself in, an interesting hole I find myself in, fits me rather neatly, doesn't it? In fact it fits me staggeringly well, must have been made to have me in it!" This is such a powerful idea that as the sun rises in the sky and the air heats up and as, gradually, the puddle gets smaller and smaller, it's still frantically hanging on to the notion that everything's going to be all right, because this world was meant to have him in it, was built to have him in it; so the moment he disappears catches him rather by surprise.'

This level of fascination with puddles and water, appears to never truly leave us from early childhood to adulthood. It may be because puddles are an accessible area of water, or that they are very common, so again, more accessible to all people. In the fact that they are common, we have lost the ability to see their potential.

In the poem below, we can hear from a child the potential of a puddle:

Magic Puddles by Lara Warden

Go on...

Jump In
Splash
Stir it
Race through it
Sit in it
Step over
Hop over
Leap over
Stand with your mum
Dance
Splish
Splash
Swish
Plop
Sing
Scream
Shout
Sigh

Look down under the water
Cover them
Find a friend
Find a bug
Twirl the water
Take measurements
Give it a name
Think about it
Watch it disappear
Make soup
Make perfume
Make a mess
Make a pond
Laugh
And laugh
And giggle a LOT!
All of this ...
...in a puddle

CW

In the arts

Poems by adults have been written to stimulate a desire to jump in puddles, as well as describing the nature of puddles in relation to the water cycle. The following excerpt from the poem: The Lonely Puddle by Wally Glickman, demonstrates this wonderfully:

The Lonely Puddle by Wally Glickman

Among all the lakes and the creeks and the brooks
and the streams and the rivers that water the valley
there lived a small pond,
no more than a puddle.
Rushing around her the others would babble
and clatter the pebbles and stones
and they'd giggle,
while she remained silent
and sad
and alone.

Whenever the wind would arouse her to whisper
the others continued to pay no attention.
She'd stiffen her banks feeling angry and shy,
she'd clutch at her water,
but never would cry.

The brooks and the streams always babbled of things
they had seen on their journeys,
they couldn't keep secrets.
They spoke of white snow on the peaks of high mountains,
they spoke of a lake that was known as the sea,
with waters so wide that it welcomed all rivers...
Just lies, thought the puddle,
they're lying to me.

But oh how she listened and longed just to be
a small part of what gurgled and bubbled around her.
Why couldn't she be a brook or a stream
and glide over glistening pebbles and stones
instead of a puddle, apart and alone?

There is an abundance of childrens literature and educational material available, for example, The Puddleman Storybook by Raymond Briggs (Jonathan Cape Ltd, 2004), Puddleman by Ted Staunten (Kids Can Press, 1988), and the Look Look and Look Again series by Claire Warden, Niki Buchan (Mindstretchers Ltd, 2007).

The imagery expressed through literature, poetry, fine art, theatre, music, and film of water including puddles, may be enduring, aesthetically appealing, or threatening in themselves. Alternately, water for example, the sea, may be a metaphor for birth and rebirth, violence and death, self-discovery, spiritual journey, metamorphosis, change, inspiration, and renewal. Even small areas of water that are in a puddle, offer enough stimulation that they catch our eye. The beauty of a still reflection can awaken a feeling of awe, the murky depths of a muddy puddle can ignite a mind to consider 'things' lurking in the murky depths.

Below are examples of artwork taken from the 'Water' Floorbook™ showing various children's impressions of water and puddles.

'Tadpole' by Esme Mackenzie

In ancient art, water was often represented by stylised curvilinear forms, such as the spiral or a horizontal zigzag (as found in the art of ancient Egypt). In the famed eleventh-century Bayeux Tapestry, the English Channel is represented by embroidered wavy black lines.

The brilliant Renaissance painter, sculptor, and inventor Leonardo da Vinci (1452–1519) was fascinated by water, which he described as 'vetturale di natura' (the vehicle of nature). He drew it with great precision and fine detail, examined and studied it closely, constantly in awe of its power (he had witnessed terrible floods and storms), and designed complex canal systems and locks to channel and control it.

The water world provides inspiration for folk art, art produced by mostly self-trained artists, or for the preservation of traditional ethnic cultures, including functional and decorative hand-carved wildfowl and fish decoys, decorated sea chests, ship's figureheads, and nautical ornaments. In America, the zenith of traditional folk art flourished in the nineteenth century prior to the rise of industrialisation. Traditional, Vietnamese water-puppet performances, continue a rich and ancient folk art theatre tradition, in which the puppeteers stand behind a screen in water up to their waists, with the floating bamboo water-puppet theatre occupying the middle of a pond.

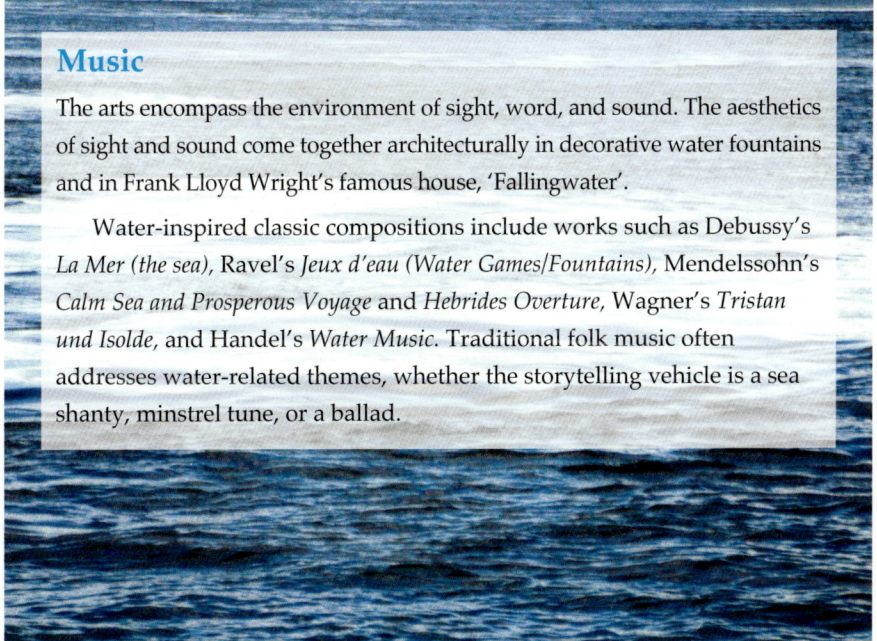

Music

The arts encompass the environment of sight, word, and sound. The aesthetics of sight and sound come together architecturally in decorative water fountains and in Frank Lloyd Wright's famous house, 'Fallingwater'.

Water-inspired classic compositions include works such as Debussy's *La Mer (the sea)*, Ravel's *Jeux d'eau (Water Games/Fountains)*, Mendelssohn's *Calm Sea and Prosperous Voyage* and *Hebrides Overture*, Wagner's *Tristan und Isolde*, and Handel's *Water Music*. Traditional folk music often addresses water-related themes, whether the storytelling vehicle is a sea shanty, minstrel tune, or a ballad.

Chapter 2. Case Studies with Analysis and Possible Lines of Development

Case Study 1: The REAL potential of a puddle!

On the rainiest day of the year, two 4 year old boys decided to explore some puddles. This is their story …

In a part of our garden, there are a whole series of puddles left over from various digging experiments of the past. Two boys were drawn to this area, and they were off to 'test the puddles'.

To begin with, the boys were a little cautious, so they carried out mini-risk / wellie (rubber rain boots), depth assessments. They would enter slowly from the side and move across the puddle to check the depth right into the middle. Once they were sure that the puddle was not too deep, they would jump in.

We started to talk about how deep the puddles were:

> "It's okay, none of these go over your wellies
> (rubber rain boots)."

Adult: "How do we know how deep it is?"

> "We could check it with a stick!"

Then, one of the boys got a very short stick, and it
went in up to his hand.

> "This stick's too small, I need a bigger one."

"Wow! That's pretty deep–nearly half the stick."

> *"I know, I'm 'gonna' test it with me.*
> *Yep, it's not over my wellies–it's*
> *not that deep."*

The boys then moved around the puddles, exploring depths and testing with sticks and other items. One of the boys, then noticed that some of the things were floating in the water and started to discuss this with his friend.

"Look! Our measuring stick floats, and those leaves."

"But that one is sinking."

"It's 'cause you splashed it with water and it got heavy."

"Let's try a new leaf, be careful putting it in."

"I'll try these little ones."

"Let's try a stone."
"Agh! That just sunk."

"Watch this big one."
"Wow, big splash! Where did it go?"

The boys then fished around using their measuring stick and eventually, somehow found it, and dragged it to the side.

"There it is, let's try again."

"What about this? This will float."

They then tried a wood 'cookie' that was the same size as the stone, but made of wood.

The boys then moved out of the woodland cover into the garden, and discovered two things about the next puddle.

"Look, I can see me! And there are bubbles. Where are the bubbles from?"

The boys moved to see their reflection move and kept on staring at the bubbles.

"The rain is splashing and it turns into a bubble, look, and now it's gone!"

"It only lasts a minute–why is that?"

"It's not washing up liquid, it's just natural in there."

The boys then checked to see if the other puddles had bubbles and discovered it was only the ones in the garden, not under the trees. They thought it could be due to the size and so measured a few puddles.

"No, these are the same as over there."

Adult: "Is there anything above us here in the garden compared to over there in the wood?"

"There is just sky here, there are trees there."

Adult: "So do you think that makes a difference to how the rain drop falls in the puddle?"

"I don't know ... "

The boys went off to explore more about puddles and what they could put in them.

The next day we reflected upon what we had learned about puddles in the camp journal and talked more about these strange bubbles. We decided to watch the puddles on a different day, when it wasn't raining quite so hard, to see what happened and if the bubbles were there.

Analysis of learning

The boys explored many aspects of puddles; their shape, size and depth (mathematics), reflections, floating/sinking and bubble formation (science). They spent a considerable period of time exploring these aspects and talking with each other regarding their theories and ideas. Finding the bubbles, was the only thing that confused the boys, and on that day, we didn't push the discussion, this would be a subject to explore further on other rainy days.

PLODS

1) Explore puddles on different days to see if bubbles form, where bubbles form the most, and formulate a theory as to why they form. Children may wish to create their own puddles, and try to make their own bubbles by dropping water, objects, stirring to see the link between air, gravity and water.

2) Watch puddles over a day or several days to explore how they change, linked to weather conditions and perhaps other factors. This could be done physically with chalk, flour or string, for marking boundaries, or photographically.

3) Experiment further with floating and sinking using different objects and different locations. Evidence could be collected through photography or video and reflected upon at a later date.

Case Study 2: Linking puddles learning story

Two boys one aged 5 and one aged 4, decided that they wanted to make one huge puddle and would do this by cutting channels, and to link them using a spade. One of the children had had this interest whilst at nursery, several years before.

Adult: "What are you doing boys?"

"The puddles are racing, we are joining them up."

The boys then continued their discussions of where to dig to link all the puddles together. Laurie was sensibly selecting areas with the shortest distance between puddles (he knows what hard work digging is!). As he dug out the channel, the water started to flow and run from one to the other.

"This one is winning, it's going faster!" said the younger boy.

The older boy dug faster, deeper and wider to speed up the process. As the water balanced out, the flow slowed and the older boy observed:

"Look, look! This one isn't as deep as before, some water must have gone in there."

Adult: "What's your plan?"

The oldest child responded:

"To join them all up and make one big puddle."

The boys continued to create channels until all the puddles were linked.

Whilst still digging to join the puddles, the boys started to discuss and explore the stones.

Adult: "It's a bit like gold panning! What do you think you will find?"

The older boy, who had seen gold panning on the television, started to swirl his spade and keep it flat, in an attempt to sift out the stones from the mud. He then spotted two different stones.

Adult: "Ooh! That one is quartz, bright white–look."

Older boy: "I don't like that one, I like this stone, see how smooth and round it is."

Adult: "Do you think it got smoothed by the water?"

Older boy: "No, it's just like that–I'm 'gonna' take it home."

The boys continued to pan and explore the puddles and to my knowledge, they found no gold!

Analysis of learning

The boys were revisiting learning that they had undertaken in the past, building on their understanding of the properties of water and their skills of digging. The boys were highly focused and spending over an hour, with much of it independent of an adult selecting where to dig and creating their 'big puddle'. The children learnt a great deal about flow, gravity and the properties of water. They developed their skills in using the spade, both to dig and 'pan for gold'. Interest moved into the properties of soil and types of stones. This experience demonstrated excellent co-operative learning between a mixed age group, fantasy play of racing puddles, mathematics and science.

PLODS

1) Explore the properties of water further; introduce a plum line and level to explore the role of gradient in water flow. A trip can be taken to a burn (stream), or further water runways can be developed through digging them out or using pipes and gutters.

2) Investigate stones, what stones we find where, their texture, colour and so on. A Talking Tub™ could be constructed and a 3D mind map undertaken linked to stones.

3) Investigate the properties of soil and soil type. Filters can be created to separate the soil. Or, a comparison between the soil in the garden, natural river clay and commercial clays (different craft clay) can be undertaken, to explore the differences and what we can do with them.

4) Develop the idea of gold panning, allow the children to set up role-play situations, or treasure hunts. They may choose to 'plant' treasure in the soil for others to find / pan.

Case Study 3: A very rainy day... and bridges

This was a typical Scottish summers day, where the heaven's opened, two of the younger boys from camp (both aged 4), were enjoying the huge puddle that was forming outside the Kinder Kitchen. They paced through it, skipped through it, ran through, jumped in and out of it. They then started to realise for the mums and dads who didn't have wellies (rubber rain boots) on and when they arrived later to pick them up, how would they get in?

"We should make a bridge, then everyone can get in without getting wet feet."

"Where should we put it?"

"Here."

"It wobbles here, move it around."

"We need a 'measurer' to see if it is long enough."

"It's too short!"

"We can move it and add up the length, it's OK, its long enough–we can jump."

They then moved down to the bottom area near the tool working zone.

"We need another bridge–here too."

"Bricks … we can use them."

"It's too long a step, we need to move it closer. Does it wobble?"

"Move the stones underneath."

"OK, it's safe, step over."

"We need a bridge on top to go under it too. Kate hold that!" Once these bridges were complete, the boys went off to explore puddles in other parts of the garden.

Later on that day, the same two boys were creating their own role-play game linked to Peter Pan, in the sand pit (which at Auchlone is shaped like a boat, as voted for by the children).

They again returned to the theme of water and bridges:

"We need a bridge ... walk the plank. We need a bridge to get on and off the boat over the water."

The boy's collected the 'bridge' they had made earlier on, over by the Kinder Kitchen.

"This is a pirates ship, we are Peter Pan's, this is our bridge. OK, it's wobbly, we need to move it."

The boys moved the plank around the various positions, with an adult watching from a safe distance to ensure they were remembering how to stay safe.

"I will test it… hold my hand Kate, it's a little slippery."

Adult: "Why?"

"It's raining—we must be careful. We need to stop it wobbling. I will get a log."

The boys went to get a log.

"It's too short!"

"We need more. There's a gap—fill it."

The boys then made several round trips to collect the large heavy logs from the other side of the garden. As they returned, they moved the logs around under the plank to make sure they were adjusted by height, digging them in where they needed to, and constantly reminding each other to "watch your fingers", "is it wobbly?" and, "it's still slippery—stay safe".

Finally, they were happy with the stability, angle and location, and this became their access route to their ship. Other children came to join in, and the two boys showed them how to walk on the 'slippery bridge' safely.

The following day, one of the boys helped write up the learning that took place in our camp journal. He stuck in the photographs, reflected on the learning and experience of the previous day. These ideas were transcribed by a member of staff in his own words.

Analysis of learning

During this case study, the primary focus for the children was to explore access routes and different methods of crossing space. During the course of this experience, the children were constantly assessing the hazards and associated risks of the activity, and formulating their own risk assessments. The children also worked co-operatively to handle and move large planks and heavy logs into the correct location. These experiences led to some fantastic contextual learning about height, length and depth, as well as the effects of water upon wood, stone and sand.

PLODS

1) Film videos, or create photographic sequential story boarding of the children risk–assessing learning activity. These can be shown to parents, new children, or be used to remind children of the risk assessments they have undertaken, and how to safely undertake learning activities/ experiences.

2) Explore bridges and crossing methods that are familiar to children, such as, local sites and national landmarks. Look at their different construction methods and perhaps replicate styles (in model or large scale form), to explore why certain types of crossings are used in different locations. This is closely linked with the schemas of boundary and connection.

3) Undertake a planning session for real activity with the children, exploring the landscape of your site, flood zones, streams, and to see if bridges or crossing methods should be put in place. Implement decisions made through consultation.

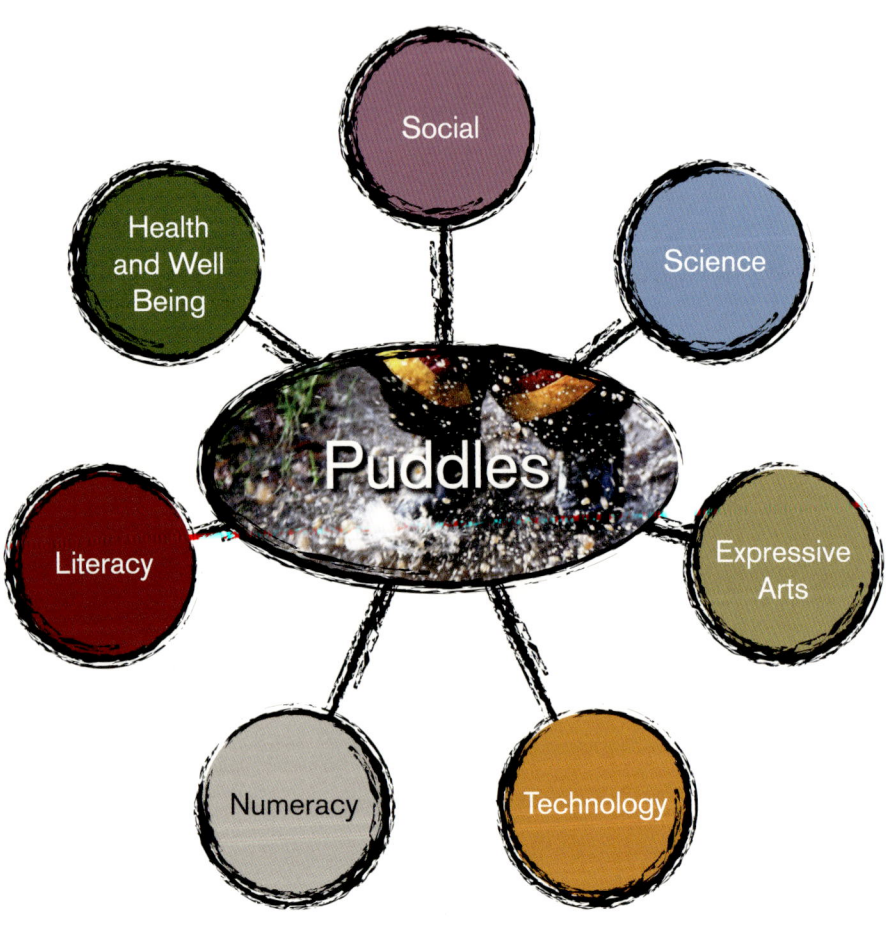

Area of enquiry
1. Conceptual knowledge about the creation of puddles (Case study 2)
2. Observations of evaporation
3. Experimenting with flotation and sinking (Case study 1)

Area of enquiry
1. Puddles as a provocation for artistic expression (Case study 1)
2. Creation of puddle painting

Area of enquiry
1. Development of technology in rain water use

Area of enquiry
1. Recording mathematical thinking
2. Encourage mathematical concepts such as shape, circumference, area and depth (Case study 1)

Area of enquiry
1. Puddles as a stimulation for different types of writing
2. Talking and listening about a puddle
3. Letter and number formation in a puddle

Area of enquiry
1. Children's awareness and management of risk (Case study 3)
2. Active outdoor learning experiences (Case study 2 & 3)
3. Water as a vital source for well being
4. Atmospheric effect of rain

Area of enquiry
1. Historical use of water by humans
2. Natural resources in the environment
3. Weather: the social and emotional link

Science

Area of enquiry concept/knowledge/skill	Opportunities for experiential learning experiences
1. Conceptual knowledge about the creation of puddles	
A puddle can be formed by either a depression in the surface or by surface tension.	Within your setting, explore areas where puddles are likely to form. Discuss why this might be. Once the rain arrives, allow children the time to observe the formation of these puddles.
A puddle can be formed naturally or by children through play.	Around the puddle, discuss how and where the water has come from. Explore natural puddles or plan and design a puddle park by changing the landscape to make depressions, embankments and canals to see if the rain fills them.
2. Observations of evaporation	
Water in a puddle can evaporate. What causes the puddle to disappear and where does the water go once it has gone?	Chalk out, or mark the area of the puddle circumference and depth. Over the session and days, return to observe the change in size and depth of your puddle. Discuss evaporation where this sits within the water cycle.
Developing knowledge on the erosive influence that water has on natural and manufactured materials, through freeze-thaw action and the force of water movement/impact.	Provide opportunities for children to explore and discover your setting, investigate signs of water erosive impact on your surrounding environment. Experiment with wood, mud, sand and metal and observe the erosive influence water has on each–this is best done seasonally to explore temperature as a parameter.

Area of enquiry concept/knowledge/skill	Opportunities for experiential learning experiences
3. Experimenting with flotation and sinking	
Objects float on water when they displace their own weight.	Allow children to experiment with different materials to investigate their flotation properties. Children will naturally place objects into a puddle and experiment with them. Provide a variety of materials for them to experiment with, and discuss with them their theories as to why this occurs.
Water can 'hold' particles (suspension).	Create opportunities for children to explore muddy water mixtures. Using clear containers will allow the children to see how the particles settle out when the water is still.

Expressive Arts	Area of enquiry concept/knowledge/skill	Opportunities for experiential learning experiences
1. Puddles as a provocation for artistic expression		
	Puddles have been used by photographers to capture the reflective properties to capture images of the world around them. Music has been used by famous artists such as Gene Kelly in the musical, 'Singin in the Rain' to express feelings and thoughts whilst dancing through rain and puddles.	Children can be given the opportunity to use cameras to capture the reflections that are found within puddles. Allow children the opportunity to dance and express themselves whilst out playing in puddles, a video camera can record this motion and be set to music later–perhaps recorded by the children. Children could also be supported to use the experience of puddles for anecdotal writing, such as, poetry about their experiences of puddles.
2. Creation of puddle painting		
	The water from puddles can be combined with plant matter, soil, berries to create natural paints, or to simply change the hue of the puddle.	Simply using the puddle as paint, using a brush, stick or finger on the ground, or on walls to create works of art. These can be photographed and reflected on, providing a rich stimulation for language. Extend through making earth coloured paints. Soil varies so much in colour from one garden to the next. The children can bring in their soil and create a varied palette of mud paint.

Area of enquiry concept/knowledge/skill	Opportunities for experiential learning experiences
1. Development of technology in rain water use	
The development of technology in harnessing rainwater, provides the opportunity to learn about industry, machinery and production methods.	Children can be given the opportunity to research the ways that people have used machines and resources to manipulate rainwater. Small rates of production using a small water mill can be compared to the mass production in industry. A water wheel can be created by children, or the power of water and how water travels, can be explored through setting up a series of pipes or gutters.

Area of enquiry concept/knowledge/skill	Opportunities for experiential learning experiences
1. Recording mathematical thinking	
The use of rain gauges between your setting and home can be used to help motivate children to engage with maths.	Create rain gauges so that the children can record precipitation within the setting, compare and contrast over a period of time, and set up as a home link to compare rainfall from setting to home.
2. Encourage mathematical concepts such as shape, circumference, area and depth	
Explore using a range of standard measuring equipment (e.g. tape measures) and non-standard (e.g. stick, hand, leaf).	Experiment with different measuring tools to record the depth of a puddle. Outlining the puddle using chalk to measure its shape and circumference, using this chalk as a measurement on how quickly evaporation occurs. Counting out or using a stop watch to record time trials, children and adults walk around the puddle to see how long it takes to do a lap around each puddle. Estimate how many buckets it takes to fill a puddle, then testing out the children's estimation. Explore the area using leaves, or other material to cover the surface.

Area of enquiry concept/knowledge/skill	Opportunities for experiential learning experiences
1. Puddles as a stimulation for different types of writing	
Children may choose to write while outside (waterproof notepads and pens), or reflect upon experience back in setting.	Using puddles as stimulation, promote children to use descriptive language or write poetry about their sensorial experiences with it. The fact that children can do so many things with water, will mean that it is a perfect object for them to use as a focus for discussion and writing.
2. Talking and listening about a puddle	
Explore feelings, factual information and even the sound effects associated with a puddle.	The experience of being around a puddle can create a calming atmosphere that supports children to take part in a range of speaking and listening activities. They can explore their reflections as they talk.
3. Letter and number formation in a puddle	
Create a mark making tool or use natural materials to make writing parchment to explore their effects in and on puddles.	Use the flat water surface as a magic writing board. Use a long stick as the writing tool. Draw letters and numbers on some leaves, put them into the puddles and float them to form words or sums.

Health and Well Being	Area of enquiry concept/knowledge/skill	Opportunities for experiential learning experiences
	1. Children's awareness and management of risk	
	Children are able to self-risk assess, and the more we can trust them to make decisions and provide supportive environments for them to do so, the more they will thrive.	Children can be supported to create their own Benefit Risk Assessment about engaging with puddles. This will encourage them to make decisions about how to look after themselves and others. The risk assessment can be written down by children, or recorded from their own words by an adult.
	2. Active outdoor learning experiences	
	Children develop fine and gross motor skills moving around, over and through puddles and outdoor spaces in their search for puddles.	Children can be encouraged to explore the outdoor area and look for puddles or signs of puddles (dry day). If there are no signs of puddles within the setting, they could be given the task of searching for puddles in their own home environment or local park, and finding out why the puddle has formed there.
	3. Water as a vital source for well being	
	Explore thirst and how much water we consume in a day. Do we know if we have drank enough to stay healthy?	Discussions on the vital need for us to have water and what the consequences are for not doing so. Encourage children to regulate their water intake, especially on warmer days. Provide access to water and allow the children to access it, as and when they require it, promoting independence but being mindful as to monitor it from a distance.
	4. Atmospheric effect of rain	
	Children enjoy the sight, sound, touch, smell and even taste of rain.	Organise a reflective discussion outside, sheltered from the rain. The soothing sound of the rain on the roof and all around, can help children to focus on the discussion of rain and create a calming atmosphere. This can be a perfect opportunity to talk about feeling and emotions to do with ourselves and each other.

Social Area of enquiry concept/knowledge/skill	Opportunities for experiential learning experiences
1. Historical use of water by humans	
Water is required by all people on the earth to survive, however, how it is used other than it being a basic requirement, varies from one culture to another, through religion, industry or recreation.	Set the children a research task using the internet, to find out how water is used by different people around the world. For example, a tip tap used in Africa can be created by the children.
2. Natural resources in the environment	
Rainwater can be a sustainable energy source if it is used sensibly and we look after it.	Research with the children why recycling rainwater in sensible quantities, can make it a sustainable resource. Create mini or large water butts and monitor the water saved.
3. Weather: the social and emotional link	
	Discuss how different weather conditions make us feel and what we do in different weather conditions. Perhaps, start to record daily weather conditions and link it with activity and emotions.

Chapter 4. Developing Skills

1. Puddle catcher

(by Steven, 33 years old)

The term puddle catcher was given to the large, black builder's tray that is at the centre. The children use it to 'puddle catch' more often than they do for mud play, due to large areas of the forest we work in that are mud pits.

1. If you do not have areas outside where puddles form naturally, you can set up the puddle catcher in your outdoor space.

2. Set out containers for the children to fill up, these can be buckets, cups, or bottles. The children fill up and then transport the water until they are happy with the level of water in the puddle.

3. The problem solving experiences to get the water from the tap to the puddle, can be extended through the provision of guttering and rods to make a frame to hold up the guttering. Extend this experience by ensuring that the bamboo guttering comes in a variety of diameters and, therefore, profiles.

4. Provide loose materials for children to place in the puddle, or ask them to go out and forage for materials in and around your setting.

5. Be mindful as they explore to pick up any fascinations that could be taken forward.

2. Water mill

(by Archie, 8 years old)

1. Collect some wood for the paddles.

2. You will need sticks to hold it together.

3. Find nails and some twine to fix the paddles in place.

4. Measure along the wood for how long you need the paddles to be, if it's too long, the paddle will get stuck, and if it's too short, the water won't reach it.

5. Once you are happy with the length of the paddle, you need to saw the wood to its size. You need to get a saw and a glove, the glove goes on your hand before you start, it goes on the hand that you're not holding the saw with.

6. Hammer your nails into the wood, and you can use twine as well to secure it if you need to.

7. Once you are finished and it's OK, go and test it out, you might need to adjust the paddles.

8. When it is working, put two sticks into the ground and place the wheel in between them. The water should push it round and round.

3. Condensation traps

(by Claire Warden)

Create a puddle from 'thin air' by creating a condensation trap.

1. Dig out a wide cone shaped hole in some damp earth.
2. Place a puddle catcher (container) in the base of the cone.
3. Suspend a plastic sheet over the whole cone area.
4. Place a stone on the plastic sheet over the container to create a drip point.
5. Leave overnight / 24 hours, so that the water evaporating from the vegetation and earth is caught on the underside of the plastic.
6. The water will dribble down the sheet and drip into the container to create a drinkable puddle!

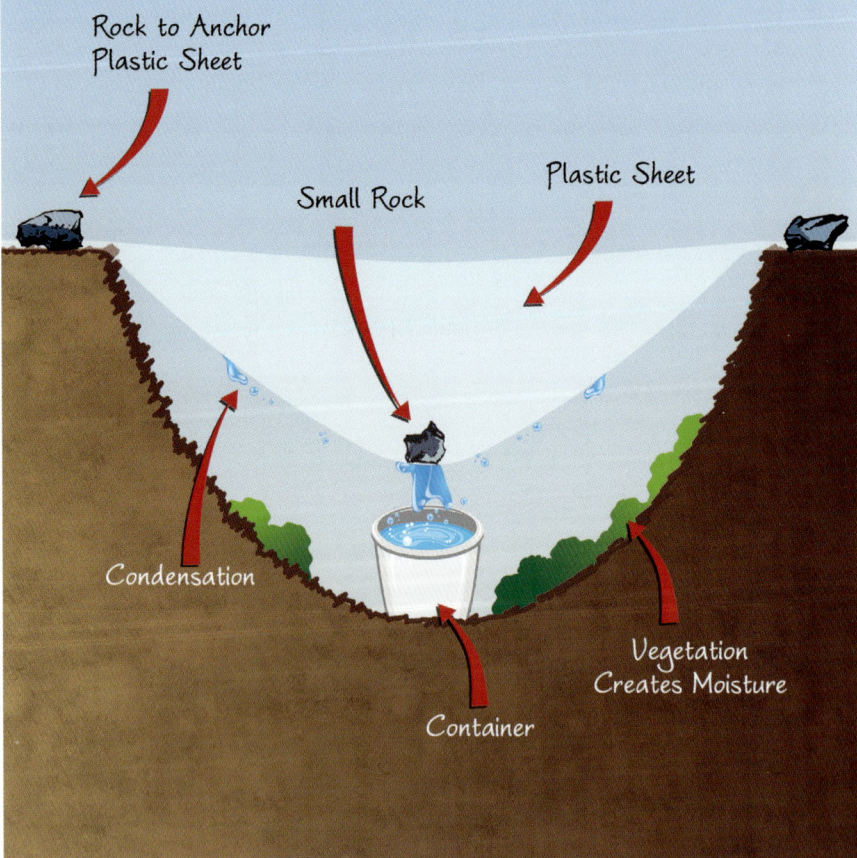

Rock to Anchor Plastic Sheet

Small Rock

Plastic Sheet

Condensation

Vegetation Creates Moisture

Container

Chapter 5. Benefit-Risk Assessment

Benefit-Risk Assessment	Water based activities
Assessment date: Aug 2012	Date for review: August 2013 - ongoing
Assessment undertaken by:	Staff member
Approved by:	Senior staff member
Local site considerations / amendments:	Unstable tree branches, low level branches, overhang area of trees. Uneven ground conditions, or obstacles on the ground. Weather effects on the ground, seating areas and other surfaces. Gradients of slope. Staff / parents / guardian and children
Benefits of activity:	• Build independence and develop trust • Group co-operation • Opportunity for participants to self-risk assess. • Build self-confidence • Group awareness • Aesthetics / spirituality / atmosphere • Understanding puddles and water cycles

Hazard	Level of risk	Precaution	Revised risk level
Drowning	Medium	• Adults are first aid trained and aware of appropriate CPR	Low
Hypothermia	Medium	• Appropriately dressed in waterproof clothing and protective footwear • Children's clothing may become soaked through, therefore, an awareness of the signs and symptoms of hypothermia must be known by all staff • Spare clothing available to change children out of wet gear and into dry • Access to a warm drink for the child to sip on • Slowly reheating a child if they become hypothermic • Warm and dry area to visit if required	Low
Medical conditions	Medium	• Allergies and medical conditions / requirements are checked prior to activity	

Hazard	Level of risk	Precaution	Revised risk level
Cuts or injuries from puddle exploration	Medium	• Cuts are washed and treated immediately, and first aid requirements dealt with appropriately	Low
Environmental impact	Medium / High	• Monitor the environmental impact upon area and desist use if causing severe damage to soil / root structures etc. • Assess if puddle source is a spring, or a depression in the ground	Low
Health hazards	Medium / High	• Contact with micro-organism • Stagnant water to be checked for signs of pollutant or life	Low

Summary

The journey to see the potential of a puddle has now hopefully begun. The next time it rains or the water overflows, hopefully, the reader will see it as a moment of such opportunity for learning, that he or she will not be able to resist. The nature of learning, is that it happens for children when they are afforded the opportunity to engage in an environment that respects their motivation. Children have many childhood rights, one of them, surely, has to be the joy of jumping in a puddle, having said that, adults who work with children should have playfulness in their hearts, so that they can hold an understanding of the attraction.

With kind regards

C. Warden.

Do keep in touch through **www.claire-warden.com**

or through the publishers **www.mindstretchers.com**

Mindstretchers Publications

A new series of books that provide an insight into the knowledge you need as an adult to facilitate learning occurring in outdoor environments. Includes case studies with analysis and Possible Lines of Development (P.L.O.D) with full colour photography throughout.

'The true value of this little gem of a book is that it respects the power of allowing children to have their own adventures, follow their own imaginations and make their own discoveries.' Tim Gill

'An invaluable and inspirational resource, by an internationally recognized expert in her field, that beautifully illustrates the power of nature to amplify every dimension of learning.' Richard Louv

A series of 4 Fascinations: Fire; Earth; Water; Air.

E-book versions available (EPUB and Kindle) **visit www.mindstretchers.com for worldwide online retail outlets.**

To find out more about Claire Warden's books visit **www.claire-warden.com** or go to **www.mindstretchers.com** to order online.

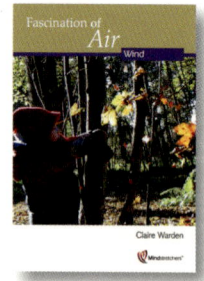

Published by

Mindstretchers™

Email enquiries@mindstretchers.co.uk

Tel +44(0)1764 664 409 **Fax** +44(0)1764 660 728

Inspirational Learning, Inside, Outside and Beyond